WILDLY GROSS

Why did Karen Carpenter give her dog away?

It kept trying to bury her.

What is 5-12-6?

The measurements of Miss Somalia.

What has four wheels and flies?

A dead cripple in a wheelchair.

What do Ethiopians and Yoko Ono have in common?

They both live off dead beetles.

WILDLY GROSS JOKES

by Julius Alvin

ZEBRA BOOKS
KENSINGTON PUBLISHING CORP.

ZEBRA BOOKS are published by

Kensington Publishing Corp.
850 Third Avenue
New York, NY 10022

First Printing: July, 1996
10 9 8 7 6 5 4 3 2 1

Printed in the United States of America

For J.J.

Contents

Wildly Gross

What do you call an epileptic in a vegetable garden?

A seizure salad.

A young man goes to see his shrink and says, "Doc, you just got to help me. Every night I have the same dream: I'm lying in bed and five gorgeous women come in, try to tear my clothes off, and have wild sex with me."

"And what do you do?" the shrink asks.

"I push them away," the young man says.

"And what do you want me to do?" the shrink asks the young man.

"Break my arms!"

What do you get when you mix orange juice and milk of magnesia?

A Phillips screwdriver.

What do you call a gay dwarf?

A low blow.

YOU KNOW YOU'RE WHITE TRASH WHEN . . .

Your children have head lice as pets.

Your neighbors spray their phone with Lysol after you use it.

Your parents share the same set of false teeth.

Your IQ and your wife's bra size are the same.

You set your bed on fire trying to light your farts.

Your sister used to date Lobster Boy.

Your idea of a wet dream is winning a case of Budweiser.

You kiss your grandmother and she slips you the tongue.

You blow your entire welfare check on lottery tickets.

Hear about the Polish employee?

They wanted to pay him what he was worth, but he wouldn't work that cheap.

Hear about the Polish loser?

His swimming pool burned down.

How do you know when your marriage is in trouble?

On your wedding night, she says, "I think we're seeing too much of each other."

How do you know when you're a loser?

You join the KKK and they burn a cross on *your* lawn.

A man goes to see his physician and says, "Doc, you won't believe this, but every time I sneeze, I have an incredible orgasm. What do you recommend?"

The doctor replies, "Black pepper."

Here's the bad news: Adolf Hitler is still alive and is living in Argentina.

Here's the good news: He's finally going to be tried for all his crimes against humanity.

Here's the worse news: He's being tried in L.A.

What do you call it when your girlfriend puts ice cream on her twat?

Hair pie a la mode.

What's the best way to avoid rape?

Beat off your attacker.

Two young brothers, aged five and six, are listening through the keyhole as their older sister is getting it on with her boyfriend.

They hear her say, "Oh, Jim, you're going where no man has gone before!"

The six-year-old says to his brother, "He must be fucking her up the ass!"

What's the difference between an Italian woman and a bowling ball?

You can eat a bowling ball.

A man goes to a prostitute and hands her the agreed-upon fee of fifty dollars.

Getting undressed, the hooker asks him, "What would you like to do?"

The man replies, "I'd really like to have wild sex, and then spank you."

The hooker asks, "How long do you want to spank me?"

The man replies, "As long as it takes to get my fifty dollars back."

The marriage counselor asked the husband, "Why did you throw apples at your wife when you had your last fight?"

"Because," the husband replied, "watermelons were out of season."

What's gay and jerks off into washing machines?

The Mayfag repairman.

What do a priest and a Christmas tree have in common?

They both have balls that are just for decoration.

It's Joe's turn to have the guys over for poker. Unfortunately, his wife has to work late and he can't find a babysitter for his twelve-year-old son, Joe Junior.

The kid is annoying everyone, walking around the poker table and yelling out which cards the men are holding. Joe and his buddies are getting fed up, because every time Joe chases his son away, the kid always comes back and continues yelling out the different hands.

Finally, Joe grabs his son and takes him into the bathroom, then comes back to the table and picks up his cards. Half an hour later, one of the guys remarks, "Hey, Joe—where's your kid? We ain't seen him in a while. What did you do, kill him?"

"Nah," Joe replies. "I taught the kid how to jerk off."

What's blue and comes in brownies?

Cub scouts.

Why do mutes masturbate with only one hand?

So they can moan with the other.

What's the definition of an Indian agent?

Someone who only takes ten percent of your scalp.

What's the difference between a porcupine and Congress?

Porcupines have their pricks on the outside.

What is a transvestite's philosophy of life?

"Eat, drink, and be Mary."

Three Doberman pinschers are sitting in their individual cages at the veterinarian's office. The first Doberman says to the second, "What are you in for?"

The first Doberman replies, "I was humping my master's leg so often, he decided to bring me here and have my pecker whacked off What are you in for?"

The first Doberman replies, "Same thing."

The second Doberman turns to the third Doberman and asks, "So what are you in for?"

"Well," says the third Doberman, "my mistress is this really hot-looking woman. Last night she came out of the shower, naked as the day she was born. When she bent over to put on her panties, I just couldn't help myself. I ran up behind her and rammed myself into her sweet little snatch."

"So I guess you're here to get your pecker whacked off, too?" asks the second Doberman.

"Hell no," says the third. "I'm in here to get my teeth cleaned and my toenails clipped."

The day after the wedding, the groom called his best friend and confessed that the wedding night had been something of a disaster.

"We made love, sure," said the groom to his buddy, "but out of habit, after we were done, I took fifty dollars and left it on her pillow."

"What's so bad about that?" the best friend asked.

"Well," the groom replied, "she said she usually gets a hundred."

"Sex is a driving force in my marriage," one man says to his friend at the golf course.

"Is that a fact?" asks his friend.

"Yes," replies the first. "She's always telling me to stop and ask for directions."

The couple had been married for thirty years. One night, the husband is reading the newspaper and announces to his wife, "It says here in the paper that in Turkey, women pay their men fifty dollars to have sex. I'm leaving you and moving to Turkey."

His wife replies, "I'd like to come along."

"Why?" he asks.

"I'd like to see you live on fifty dollars a year," his wife says.

What do you get when you stuff french fries up your girlfriend's twat?

Fish and chips.

You know a woman is ugly when . . .

1. She looks out the window and gets arrested for mooning.

2. As a baby, she had to be breast-fed by the family dog.

3. Even mosquitoes won't bite her.

4. She goes to the zoo and scares all the animals.

5. The tide won't even take her out.

6. On Halloween, she has to trick-or-treat over the phone.

7. She makes onions cry.

8. Her butt looks like two pigs fighting over a box of Milk Duds.

9. Her armpits look like she has Don King in a headlock.

10. The plastic surgeon wanted to add a tail.

Why does a bald man have a hole in his pants pocket?

So he can scratch his hair now and then.

Where do rich black folks live?

In coon-dominiums.

Why does it take four women with PMS to screw in a lightbulb?

IT JUST DOES, OKAY?

A man walks into a saloon, puts his briefcase down on the bar, and orders a shot. He asks the bartender if he can have a tiny shot for his friend. He opens the briefcase and inside is a little man, one-foot tall, sitting at a tiny piano playing tunes.

The bartender is amazed. "Where did you find him?"

The guy says, "I made a wish to the genie in this lamp." He pulls a magic lamp out of his briefcase and puts it on the bar.

"Can I make a wish?" the bartender wants to know, and the guy says, "Sure, go ahead."

The bartender rubs the magic lamp and says, "I wish I had a million bucks."

In a flash the saloon is filled with a million quacking ducks, from floor to ceiling.

The bartender starts screaming, "I said a million *bucks,* not a million *ducks!* Is this genie deaf or something?"

The lamp's owner screams back, "Hey, what do you think, that I asked for a twelve-inch *pianist?*"

Gross Celebrity Jokes

What did the seven dwarfs say when the prince woke Sleeping Beauty up?

"Looks like it's back to jerking off"

What do Roseanne and a football have in common?

Pigskin.

How do you know Roseanne is really fat?

She hangs license plates from her charm bracelet.

If Tarzan was an Arab, what would Cheetah be?

Pregnant.

Why does Stevie Wonder have one black leg and one yellow leg?

His dog is blind, too.

Why doesn't Roseanne ever wear yellow?

So people will stop thinking she's a taxi.

What does Michael Jackson hate about having sex?

Getting the bubble gum off his dick.

Hear about the new movie with Michael Jackson?

Close Encounters of the Third Grade.

What's the difference between Jane Fonda and Bill Clinton?

Jane Fonda went to Vietnam.

What do Ethiopians and Yoko Ono have in common?

They both live off dead beetles.

What's the difference between Madonna and a limousine?

Not everyone's been in a limousine.

What do you call a bathroom for bisexuals?

The Elton John.

Michael Jackson goes to see his doctor for a checkup. After the examination, the doctor says to him, "Mr. Jackson, have you been having sex with little boys again?"

"Yes," Michael Jackson confesses, "but I just can't help myself. But how did you know?"

The doctor replies, "Because you've got a G.I. Joe doll up your ass."

What do Jeffrey Dahmer and gravediggers have in common?

They both dig dead people's holes.

What's the difference between Pee Wee Herman and Rodney King?

Pee Wee only beats himself.

A very rich man suffers a heart attack and is rushed to the hospital. A few days later, his doctor comes to him and says, "I have good news and I have bad news."

"What's the good news?" the rich man wants to know.

"The good news is," the doctor says, "your heart attack isn't as bad as we first thought, and with some rest and a proper diet, you'll recover very nicely."

"That *is* good news," the rich man says. "But what's the bad news?"

"The bad news is," the doctor says, "your wife just fired me and hired another doctor named Kevorkian."

How does Ted Bundy's family honor his memory?

Every year they put a wreath on a fusebox.

What did Jodie Foster say to her girlfriend?

"My face or yours?"

What does Jodie Foster do every day at noon?

She has a box lunch.

Hear about Evel Knievel's latest stunt?

He's going to run across Somalia with a sandwich tied to his back.

What do you call Jodie Foster, k.d. lang, and Martina Navratilova?

A menage-a-twat.

What's the difference between Hillary Clinton and a great white shark?

Nail polish.

What do you get when you cross a cat with Mick Jagger?

A pussy with big lips.

What's brown and hides in an attic?

The Diarrhea of Anne Frank.

Why did Maria Shriver marry Arnold Schwarzenegger?

They're trying to breed bulletproof Kennedys.

Hear about the new special sandwich at McDonald's?

It's called a McJackson—35-year-old meat between 11-year-old buns.

What has 200 legs and ten teeth?

The front row of a Willie Nelson concert.

What does Tailhook really stand for?

"Do we have to do it doggy-style again, Admiral?"

How did Helen Keller's parents punish her?

They stretched Saran Wrap over the toilet.

How does Helen Keller masturbate?

She gets a manicure.

Why did Karen Carpenter give her dog away?

It kept trying to bury her.

Why was Oprah Winfrey arrested for drug possession?

Cops found fifty pounds of crack under her dress.

What do you get when you cross a Jew with Ted Kennedy?

A drunk who buys his booze retail.

What's so special about the White House elevator?

It's the only thing Hillary Clinton will go down on.

Gross Ethnic Jokes

Hear about the lazy Polack?

He fell asleep during his nap.

Hear about the lazy Polish bank-robber?

He faxed the stick-up note to the teller.

What's the definition of gross stupidity?

The population of Poland.

Hear about the Polish twins?

They kept forgetting each other's birthday.

Hear about the Polish Olympic team?

They had their gold medals bronzed.

Hear about the Polish poker player?

He wore black gloves so nobody could see his hand.

How dumb was the Polish woman?

She had to take her bra off to count to two.

What's black and crispy and sits on your roof?

An Italian electrician.

Why did the Italian organ grinder always keep his monkey around?

Someone had to do the books.

Who really assassinated John F. Kennedy?

Four hundred Polish sharpshooters.

A Polish boy goes to a whorehouse to lose his virginity. His friend tells him to ask for 69.

The Polish boy says to the whore, "I'd like 69." She agrees.

Before she can stick her twat in his face, though, she lets loose a huge fart. She opens the window to let the stink out. But before she can get back on top of him, she lets out another huge fart, and crosses to the window to air out the room again. With this, the Polish kid gets up and puts his clothes back on.

"Where are you going?" the hooker wants to know.

The Polish kid says, "If you think I'm hanging around for 67 more of your farts, you're crazy."

What did Jesus Christ say to the Polish people as he was hanging on the cross?

"Play dumb till I get back."

A black guy and a Puerto Rican guy are in a car. Who's driving?

The cop.

What's the toughest part about being a successful black businessman?

Fitting the watermelon in his briefcase.

What do you call a Jewish American princess in a basement?

A whine cellar.

Why did the black guy have a heart attack on Halloween?

Someone came to his door dressed as a job.

Why do Mexicans eat so many beans?

So they can take bubble baths later.

What do you call a constipated Chinaman?

Hung Chow.

A socially conscious couple decided they wanted to help humanity, so they went into Harlem and found a homeless black woman. They brought her home, with the understanding that she would do housework and get paid for her efforts.

Two weeks later, the black woman went to her employers and informed them that she was pregnant. What choice did they have but to stick by her? Three weeks after giving birth, the black woman informed them that she was pregnant again.

The white couple adopted the second child as well. Three weeks later, the black woman informed the couple that she was pregnant for a third time.

"Also," she told them, "I is quitting."

"Quitting?" the husband asked, clearly shocked. "Buy why?"

"I agreed to do some cookin' and cleanin'," the black woman said, "but you didn't say nothin' 'bout working for a family with three kids!"

Why do blacks have big lips?

So they can suck change out of parking meters.

What's the difference between a black and a Polack?

A black takes the dishes out of the sink before he pisses into it.

How do you get twenty Haitians into a paper cup?

Tell them it floats.

What do you call a Mexican in a Cadillac?

Grand theft auto.

A Polack walks into a travel agency and asks for the hundred-dollar trip to nowhere. The travel agent takes his money and hits him over the head with a blackjack, then drags him into the back room.

An hour later, a Puerto Rican walks into the same travel agency and likewise asks for the hundred-dollar trip to nowhere. Again, the travel agent hits the Puerto Rican over the head with a blackjack and drags him into the back room.

Hours later, the two men wake up in a tiny rowboat in the middle of the Atlantic Ocean. The Puerto Rican says to the Polack, "Do they serve drinks on this trip?"

The Polack replies, "They didn't last year."

What do you call an Iraqi who practices birth control?

A humanitarian.

What's the most popular game show in Israel?

"The Price is Right."

Sam and Myron were gin rummy partners for years—until Sam discovered his wife in bed with Myron.

"Look," Sam says to his friend Myron. "I know you've been screwing my wife, but I still love her. This is what we'll do. We'll play one hand of gin rummy, and whoever wins gets to keep her."

"Fine," Myron agrees. "But just to keep it interesting, let's play for a penny a point."

How do Jews celebrate Christmas?

They put parking meters on their roofs.

What do you call a taco with a food stamp in it?

A Mexican fortune cookie.

What is 5-12-6?

The measurements of Miss Somalia.

Who killed more Indians than Custer?

Union Carbide.

Don Minnestrone, the most feared Mafia boss in the United States, calls his driver, Tony, into his office.

"Will you do anything for me, Tony?" the Godfather asks his driver.

"Yes, Don Minnestrone," Tony says.

"I want you to take this paper cup and masturbate into it," the Godfather tells him.

Tony shrugs, goes into the bathroom, and jerks off into a cup.

When he comes out, the Godfather says to him, "Will you do anything for me, Tony?"

"Yes Godfather," Tony replies. "Anything."

"Good," says the Godfather. "I want you to go back into the bathroom and jerk off into another cup."

Tony dutifully obeys, and jerks off into a cup a second time. When he comes out, Don Minnestrone says to him, "Will you do anything for me, Tony?"

"Yes, Godfather," Tony says. "Anything."

Once again, the Godfather tells Tony to go into the bathroom and masturbate into a cup. Tony comes out, looking exhausted.

"Are you tired, Tony?" the Godfather asks his driver.

"Very," Tony replies.

"Good," the Godfather says. "Now you can drive my daughter to the airport."

What kind of identification do Jewish mothers carry in their purses?

A card that reads, "In case of accident, I'm not surprised."

What did the Jewish burglar say to the terrified store owner?

"Give me all your money or I'll mark down every item in the store by fifty percent."

Epstein took his sales force out to dinner and said to them, "In any business, there are a million ways to make a fortune, but only one honest way."

"And what would that be, Mr. Epstein?" one of the salesman asked.

Epstein said, "How the hell should I know?"

Hear about the Jewish baseball player?

Every time he stole a base, he felt guilty and went back.

Why was the Polish kid named "Seven and one-half?"

His mother picked his name out of a hat.

Why did the slave traders bring black people to America?

So Indians could hate them, too.

Why is the NFL painting all their footballs green?

Ever hear of a black guy dropping a watermelon?

More Gross Ethnic Jokes

Why do blacks hate square dancing?

Every time someone yells "hoe-down" they think one of their bitches has been shot.

Why are Mexicans like playing pool?

You have to keep hitting them to get any English out of them.

How are a black scholar and a pound of uncooked hamburger alike?

They're both very rare.

What do you call one white guy with three black guys?

Victim.

What are the words white people fear the most?

"We be yo' new neighbors."

What's transparent and hangs out in a gutter?

An Arab with the shit kicked out of him.

What does a black parrot say?

"Polly want a white ho."

What do you get when you cross a black man and a Jew?

A janitor in a law firm.

What does a Jewish bird call sound like?

"Cheap cheap cheap!"

What do you get when you cross an Italian with a Polack?

A hit man who misses.

Epstein is on his honeymoon in Atlantic City. Something of a ladies' man, Epstein can't resist getting some extra action, even though he's only been married for 24 hours.

On the second night of the honeymoon, after making love to his wife, Epstein goes for a stroll along the boardwalk and meets an attractive prostitute.

"How much?" he asks the whore.

"A hundred dollars," she replies.

"Too much," Epstein says. "How about fifty?"

"Are you kidding?" the whore replies, and brushes him off.

The next evening, Epstein and his new bride are strolling together along the boardwalk, and pass by the prostitute he had talked to the night before.

Seeing them, the whore yells out to Epstein, "See what you get for fifty dollars, cheapskate?"

What do you call a black man sitting on a horse?

LeRoy Rogers.

What happened to the Polack who put Odoreaters in his shoes?

He took three steps and disappeared.

Why did the Polish woman stick a lit candle in her twat?

Her boyfriend liked to eat by candlelight.

Hear about the ugly Polish kid?

Her parents hired another girl to play her in home movies.

What's the German word for Ky-Jelly?

Derweinerslider.

What do you call two Italian women taking a shower?

Gorillas in the Mist.

What did the doctor say to the Polish woman after she gave birth?

"Lady, if it doesn't start crying in ten seconds, it's a tumor."

How do you know when a Polish woman is really stupid?

She has to take off her blouse to count to two.

Two Polish men are hiking in the woods. One of them points and says to the other, "Look, there's a dead bird!"

The second Polack looked up.

First Polack: "My car just got stolen!"

Second Polak. "You better call the police, quick."

First Polack: "That's okay. I got the license plate number."

How did the Polack get brain-damaged?

A piece of paper fell on his head.

What's a Polack's favorite deodorant?

RAID.

How do you know Harlem is so dangerous?

Even the cockroaches wear bulletproof vests.

How do you know Detroit is really dangerous?

The milk cartons have pictures of missing cops on them.

Why is an Italian woman like a nail?

She likes to get hammered.

"I think my wife is being unfaithful to me," one Italian guy said to his friend.

"How do you figure?" his friend asked.

The first Italian guy said, "She keeps a changemaker in her pantyhose."

Why is a Jewish-American princess like an elephant?

She rolls on her back for peanuts.

Now That's Sick!

What did Henry the Eighth say to his lawyer?

"Screw the alimony. I've got a better idea."

What do you get when you have sex with a canary?

Twerpies.

What is 69 and 69?

Dinner for four.

Five-year-old Timmy goes into the bathroom, where his mother, stark naked, is just getting out of the bathtub.

Pointing to her pubic hair, he asks, "Mommy, what's that?"

Embarrassed, his mother replies, "That's where Daddy hit Mommy with an ax."

"No shit?" Timmy asks, astonished. "Right in the cunt?"

Why do hunters make the best lovers?

Because they go deep into the bush, always shoot more than once, and always eat what they shoot.

Two rednecks are out duck hunting, when suddenly a huge flock comes flying overhead. Jim Bob shoulders his rifle, aims, and fires. A big fat duck lands inches from where they are standing.

"Great shot, eh, Clem?" Jim Bob asks proudly.

"Great shot nothing," Clem replies. "You wasted a bullet."

"How do you figure that?" Jim Bob wants to know.

"Hell," Clem says. "The fall alone would've killed him."

The attractive French gal walked into the waterfront saloon in New York City and said to a sailor, "I'm broke, and I have no way of getting back to Paree."

The sailor said to her, "I think I have an idea. We're shipping out for France in an hour. I can smuggle you onboard the ship, hide you, and bring you food every day until we dock. There's just one thing you have to do for me."

"What's that?" Fifi asks.

"Each day at ten in the morning and three in the afternoon, you have to have sex with me."

Fifi agrees, and the sailor smuggles her aboard and stashes her in a supply closet. As promised, the sailor brings her food every day, and Fifi has sex with him promptly at ten and three o'clock.

On the seventh day of the voyage, the sailor doesn't show up. Fifi, afraid of starving to death, leaves the supply closet and goes out on deck. She finds a man who looks like the captain of the ship, and confesses everything.

"France?" the captain asks, astonished. "Lady, I don't know what that sailor told you, but this boat ain't going to France. You're on the Staten Island Ferry."

What's the definition of group sex?

Masturbating with both hands.

The middle-aged woman comes home from her checkup, grinning from ear to ear. Her husband asks, "What are you smiling about?"

The wife answers, "The doctor says I have the bust of a woman half my age. Isn't that sweet?"

"What did he say about your big fat, fifty-year-old ass?"

"Your name didn't come up," the wife says.

What is 6.9?

Something great, broken up by a period.

What's better than playing the piano by ear?

Fiddling with your dick.

What do you call a stork who delivers babies in Alabama?

A dope peddler.

Why did the guy from Alabama walk around with his dick hanging out?

So he could count to eleven.

The redneck goes to the doctor because he's constipated. The doctor prescribes a powerful laxative and tells the redneck to come back in three days for another checkup.

When the redneck comes back, the doctor asks him, "Have you moved yet?"

The redneck says he hasn't, so the doctor writes him out a prescription for a laxative that's twice as strong as the first.

"Come back in three days," the doctor tells him.

Three days later, the redneck is back.

The doctor asks, "Have you moved yet?"

The redneck says he still hasn't, so the doctor gives him a prescription for a laxative three times as strong as the first two. Three days later, the redneck comes back, and this time he's smiling.

"Can I safely assume that you've moved?" the doctor asks him.

The redneck nods and says, "I had to. My double-wide was full of shit!"

What happened when the prostitute got leprosy?

Business started falling off.

What do you call a leper in a bathtub?

Stew.

What did the leper do when the other driver cut him off?

He gave him the finger.

Six-year-old Suzy runs into the house, all out of breath, and asks her mother, "Mommy, can little girls have babies?"

"Why, heavens no," her mother responds.

"Thanks," Suzy says, and as she runs out the door, she calls to her friends, "It's okay. We can play that game again!"

Redneck girl to her mother: "Ma, I think I'm pregnant."

Mother: "Don't worry, maybe it isn't yours."

Hear about the Polish abortion clinic?

There's a twelve-month wait.

How do you make a Puerto Rican?

Sandblast a nigger.

What do you call six lesbians in a hot tub?

A clambake.

How do hookers clean their teeth in Los Angeles?

With dental Fleiss.

Why did the redneck stop moving his bowels?

He was afraid he'd forget where he left them.

What's the difference between Saddam Hussein and a bag of shit?

The bag.

What's the definition of "mixed emotions?"

Seeing your mother-in-law go over a cliff in your Corvette.

Hear about the man who went to spend a week in a nudist colony?

His first day was his hardest.

What's three miles long and has an IQ of ten?

The St. Patrick's Day Parade.

Gross Gay and Lesbian Jokes

What do you call a gay masochist?

A sucker for punishment.

Why do fags grow moustaches?

To hide their stretchmarks.

The state trooper was patrolling a country road when he spotted a man tied to a tree—stark naked.

"What happened here?" the trooper asked the naked man.

"Well," the man said, "I picked up a hitchhiker, and as soon as he got into the car, he pulled a gun, took my money, made me take off all my clothes, then did this to me!"

The trooper unzipped his fly and said, "Boy, this just ain't your day."

The fag had a bad case of hemorrhoids, so his doctor gave him suppositories. When it came time to use them, though, the fag was nervous about putting them in properly. So he bent over, looking through his legs at the mirror to get a better view of his asshole.

Suddenly, his dick started getting hard and blocked his view of the mirror.

"Oh, stop it," the fag said to his penis. "It's only me."

How do straight men suddenly turn gay?

They get sucked into it.

How many queers does it take to screw in a lightbulb?

None. Queers don't screw. They butt-fuck.

Bruce and Stanley were returning home from their favorite gay bar late one night. Bruce said, "Are you hungry, Stanley?"

"Now that you mention it," Stanley replied, "I am."

Just as that point, a flasher bounded out from the alley and exposed himself.

"Perfect," Bruce said. "Take-out food!"

Why are there so many homosexuals in the world?

Because there's a sucker born every minute.

Why was the gay Mexican fisherman so depressed?

He couldn't stop thinking about the Juan who got away.

A swishy fag walks into the toughest, meanest truck stop on the highway. Sitting on his shoulder is a canary.

The place is full of burly, muscular truckers. The fag announces, "Whoever can guess the weight of the canary on my shoulder gets to take me into the back room and fuck me up the ass!"

One trucker calls out, "Five hundred pounds."

The fag says, "Folks, we have a winner!"

Two faggots are driving home one night in a blinding rainstorm and don't see the truck ahead of them stop short. The fag behind the wheel crashes into the truck. The trucker climbs out of the rig, hopping mad, and begins screaming at the gay driver.

"You stupid son-of-a-bitch, you drive like shit! You can kiss my rosy red ass!"

The gay driver says to his companion, "Thank God. He wants to settle out of court."

How do you make a fruit cordial?

Pat him on the ass.

Why was the fag disappointed when he finally arrived in London?

He found out Big Ben was actually a clock.

What did one gay sperm say to the other gay sperm?

"How am I supposed to find the egg in all this shit?"

What did the lesbian say as she guided her girlfriend's tongue to her clitoris?

"This bud's for you."

Bonnie walks into a bar with some time to kill, and orders a beer. When her eyes adjust to the dimness, she realizes with some horror that she's just entered a dyke bar.

Sure enough, a big lezzie spots her and starts coming on to her. She's chagrined to learn that Bonnie is straight.

"Men," the big lezzie snorts. "My dildo can do anything a man can do!"

"Oh yeah?" Bonnie asks. "Let's see it get up and order a round for the house."

Hear about the gay plastic surgeon?

He hung himself.

What do you call a bouncer in a gay bar?

A flamethrower.

Why did the fag join the Navy?

He wanted to be a rear admiral.

What do you call a fag with a chipped front tooth?

An organ grinder.

What do you call two fags named Bob?

Oral Roberts.

How did the two fags in the gay bar settle their argument?

They went out into the alley and exchanged blows.

Why did the lesbian return home from her European vacation a week early?

She missed her native tongue.

What's the difference between an elephant and a bulldyke?

A hundred pounds and a flannel shirt.

The insurance salesman was writing up a policy for the fag. The salesman said, "So you want your policy to be straight life, right?"

"Well," said the fag, "I *would* like to play around on Saturday nights."

A fag walks into a rough waterfront bar and propositions a sailor. The sailor is straight, so he drags the fag into the alley and beats the living crap out of him.

A policeman walks by and sees the dazed fag lying in the alley. He says to the fag, "Jesus, what happened to you? You're all black and blue. I better take you home."

"Oh, don't do that," the fag pleads. "I'll clash with my curtains."

Hear about the gay mafia Godfather?

The kiss of death includes dinner and dancing.

What happens when you get mugged by a gang of fags?

Two of them hold you down and the third does your hair.

A Gross Variety

Why did the ugly girl swallow a pin?

So she would know what it felt like to have a prick inside her.

The ventriloquist had been unemployed for months and was thrilled to finally get a job in a small Alabama town at a local theater.

All was going well until the ventriloquist started doing a lot of hillbilly jokes. Finally, one redneck stands up and says, "We're getting tired of all these jokes. We ain't all stupid, you know."

The ventriloquist says, "I'm sorry. They're just jokes, not meant to be taken seriously."

"I ain't a-talkin' to you," the redneck says. "I'm a-talkin' to that little feller settin' on your knee."

Hear about the Polish smoke detector?

It comes with a snooze alarm.

Hear about the paranoid bloodhound?

He thought people were following him.

Every day on his lunch hour, Norman would buy a can of dog food at the supermarket, walk across the street to the park, sit on a bench, and eat it.

One day a doctor is strolling through the park and sees Norman devouring the dog food. The doctor says, "You know, that stuff isn't very good for you. In fact, a steady diet of it can kill you."

"Not to worry," Norman says. "I've been eating dog food every day for years and I'm in perfect health."

The doctor shrugs and walks away. A week later, he's walking through the park when he notices that Norman isn't around. He asks the groundskeeper where Norman is.

The groundskeeper says, "Ain't you heard? Norman died last week."

The doctor replies, "I told him eating dog food would kill him."

"Weren't the dog food," the groundskeeper says. "Norman was sitting on the curb licking his balls when a truck ran over him."

When Mrs. Johnson arrived at the doctor's office for her artificial insemination, she was shocked when the male nurse locked the door behind them and started taking off his clothes.

"Just what do you think you're doing?" she wants to know.

"Sorry, lady," the male nurse says. "We're all out of the bottled stuff, so I'll have to give you draft."

What do oral sex and a presidential debate have in common?

One slip of the tongue and you're in deep shit.

Hear about the really fat woman?

She had her own zip code.

What's the difference between a fox and a pig?

About seven beers.

What's a drunken bachelor's favorite song?

"I Never Went to Bed With an Ugly Girl, But I Sure Woke Up With a Few."

Two black guys meet on the street. Leroy says to Mojo, "I just got my first taste of pussy last night!"

"Yeah?" Mojo asks. "How did it taste?"

"Like shit," Leroy responds.

"You dumb motherfucker," Mojo says. "You took too big a bite!"

Why are men like toilets?

They're either taken or full of shit.

How do you know when you're getting old?

You're with a girl all night and the only thing that comes is the dawn.

Why do farts smell?

So deaf people can enjoy them, too.

How can you tell if your wife is being unfaithful?

You move from New York to California and you still have the same mailman.

The comedian called his wife from the road and boasted, "Last night I performed for ten minutes and got lots of laughs."

"Oh?" she asked. "Did you have sex with someone?"

Bumper sticker: "Save the whales. Harpoon Roseanne."

Why are a whiskey taster and a child molester alike?

They both like their twelve year olds.

What's the definition of a bachelor?

A man who doesn't have to leave a party just when he's beginning to enjoy himself.

What's another name for Harlem?

"Scene of the Crime."

What do you call a manhole cover in Washington, D.C.?

The entrance to the Iranian Embassy.

Why did the hooker keep failing her driver's test?

She couldn't learn to sit up straight in the car.

What did Michael Jackson say to Woody Allen?

"I'll give you two tens for a twenty."

What do you call a frozen cesspool?

Italian ices.

"My high school was so tough," one man tells his friend, "the local gangs used to steal hubcaps—off of moving cars."

"That's nothing," his friend replies. "My high school was so tough, they did abortions in biology class."

What's the definition of a black virgin?

A girl whose mother is too ugly to have a boyfriend.

Why is a pecker like a payday?

Neither one ever comes often enough.

The single guy was looking down at the end of the bar, where a really pretty chick was nursing a beer. She was wearing the tightest pair of jeans he'd ever seen.

Sitting down next to her, he asked, "Excuse me, but how does anyone get into pants that tight?"

The girl replies, "You can start by buying me a drink . . ."

What's the definition of a dummy?

A guy who rolls up his sleeve when a girl says she wants to feel his muscle.

What do Ethiopians say before picking their noses?

Grace.

Sex . . . and Other Gross Stuff

What's the definition of a loser?

A guy who puts a seashell to his ear and gets a busy signal.

Another definition of a loser?

A guy who gets AIDS from a wet dream.

What's the ultimate definition of a loser?

A guy who gets shipwrecked on a desert island . . . with his wife.

What do you have when you're holding two big green balls in your hand?

The Jolly Green Giant's undivided attention.

Then there was the proctologist who used two fingers whenever his patients wanted a second opinion.

Mike and Sam head down to Florida for spring break. Neither of them are what could be described as good-looking, but somehow, every time they went down to the beach, Sam always left with a beautiful woman, while Mike returned to the motel room alone.

"How do you manage to score all the time?" Mike wanted to know.

"It's easy," Sam told his friend. "Each day when I leave for the beach, I put on the tightest bathing suit I can find and stuff a cucumber in it."

The next day, Mike hurried down to the store and bought the tightest bathing suit he could find and a cucumber. After two days, though, he was still bombing out, while Sam was still scoring each time. Frustrated, Mike asked Sam why he wasn't scoring.

"The trunks are fine," Sam told his friend, "but tomorrow, try putting the cucumber in *front*."

What's meaner than a pit bull with AIDS?

The guy that gave it to him.

A Jew, an Indian, and a black all die and approach the pearly gates at the same time.

The Jew says, "St. Peter, I've suffered discrimination my entire life. Will I find any in heaven?"

"No," St. Peter says. "All you have to do is answer one question, and you will find peace and tranquillity for all eternity. Spell God."

"G-O-D," answers the Jew, and is admitted into heaven.

The Indian approaches St. Peter and says, "All my life I have lived on the reservation, and have known discrimination. Will there be prejudice in heaven?"

"No," St. Peter responds. "If you answer this one question correctly, peace and tranquility will be yours for all eternity. Spell God."

"G-O-D," the Indian says, and is admitted into heaven.

The black man says to St. Peter, "All my life I have lived in the ghetto and have suffered discrimination. Will I find any in heaven?"

"No," St. Peter says. "Answer this one question correctly, and peace and tranquility will be yours for all eternity. Spell cross-pollinization."

What's the definition of pussy-whipped?

Being impotent and being afraid to tell your pregnant wife.

A six-year-old boy walks into a saloon and says to the barmaid, "Give me a Scotch on the rocks."

The barmaid says, "A Scotch on the rocks? You're just a kid. Do you want to get me in trouble?"

"Maybe later," the kid replies. "In the meantime, I'd still like that drink."

What's the difference between like and love?

Spit or swallow.

Hear about the Jewish American Princess baby?

She was breast-fed by the caterer.

How do you tease your houseplants?

Water them with ice cubes.

What do you call sushi in Alabama?

Bait.

What's the best thing about dating a homeless woman?

It's easy to persuade them to spend the night with you.

What's the difference between a catfish and a lawyer?

One is a bottom-feeding, shit-sucking scavenger, the other is a fish.

"I just found out that my wife is a lesbian," Al told the bartender.

"That's too bad," the bartender said. "Are you going to divorce her?"

"Nope," Al replied. "I'm crazy about her girlfriend!"

Ed's wife is so depressed he takes her to see a psychiatrist. Ed waits outside while the shrink checks her over. Later, he calls Ed into his office.

"In my opinion," the shrink tells Ed, "your wife is depressed because she's not getting enough sex."

"What can I do?" Ed asks.

"I recommend that your wife have sex at least ten times a month," the shrink advises.

"Fair enough," says Ed. "Put me down for two."

Then there was the guy whose wife was ailing, so he took her to see the doctor. The doctor is shocked at her appearance. He says, "I don't like the looks of your wife."

"Neither do I," says her husband, "but she's great with the kids."

What's the definition of sex drive?

A condition that begins in puberty and ends at marriage.

"So let me get this straight," the prosecutor says to the defendant. "You came home from work early and found your wife in bed with a strange man?"

"That's correct," says the defendant.

"Upon which," says the prosecutor, "you took out a gun and shot your wife, killing her."

"That's correct," says the defendant.

"Then my question is," says the prosecutor, "why did you shoot your wife and not her lover?"

The defendant says, "It seemed easier than shooting a different man every day."

What's the definition of busy?

One set of jumper cables at a Mexican funeral.

Why does the Ku Klux Klan like to go surfing with black folks?

They get to hang ten.

What do you call a Mexican whore who doesn't charge?

A free-holey.

What's pink and black and hairy and sits on a wall?

Humpty Cunt.

What's the difference between having a job for ten years and being married for ten years?

After ten years, a job still sucks.

What's the hardest part of doing a sex change from a man to a woman?

Inserting the anchovies.

What's white and can be found in a woman's panties?

Clitty litter.

"Yesterday I came home from work early and found my wife in bed with my best friend," Nick said to the bartender.

"What did you do?" the bartender asked.

"I hit him on the nose with a newspaper and locked him in the basement."

"What good did that do?" asked the barkeep.

"Not much," Nick replied, "but he knew I meant business when I didn't give him his Kibbles and Bits!"

For months, Mona nagged her husband Ollie to take her to the country club so she could learn to play golf. He finally agrees, and off she goes with a set of clubs. That afternoon, Mona walks into the bar, grimacing with pain.

"So, did you enjoy your game of golf?" Ollie wants to know.

"It was horrible," Mona tells her husband. "I got stung by a bee."

"Where?"

"Between the first and second holes," she says.

"Sounds to me," Ollie replies, "like your stance was too wide."

What's the difference between a woman of forty and a man of forty?

The forty-year-old woman thinks about having kids, and the forty-year-old man thinks about dating them.

How do you know when your girlfriend is too skinny?

Her shadow weighs more than she does.

How do you know when your girlfriend is too fat?

She tries to walk down into the Grand Canyon and gets stuck.

Why is a fat woman like a moped?

They're both fun to ride until your friends see you.

What happened to the woman who went out fishing with ten men?

She came home with a red snapper.

What's a JAP's favorite book?

The Naked and the Dead.

Little Ronnie is jerking off in the bathroom when his mother walks in on him. She says, "What you're doing is wrong, Ronnie. Nice boys save it for when they're married."

A week later, Ronnie's mother asks him, "So, how are you doing with that problem we talked about last week?"

"Great, Mom," Ronnie says. "I've already saved a gallon!"

Why won't a woman win the Indianapolis 500?

She always stops to ask directions.

George is a bigshot lawyer and makes a ton of money. His wife decides she wants a maid, so he hires her one.

The next day, he calls home, and a woman answers.

"Hello," George says. "Are you the new maid?"

"Yes, sir," the maid responds.

"I would like to talk to my wife," George says.

"I'm sorry, sir," the maid says, "but she's in the bedroom having sex with the mailman."

George is furious. He says to the maid, "Having sex with the mailman, huh? Here's what I want you to do. In my study, in the top drawer of my desk, is a gun. It's already loaded. I want you to go into the bedroom and shoot my wife and the mailman."

"I can't do that," the maid says. "I'd go to jail for the rest of my life!"

"No, you won't," George assures her. "I'm the best lawyer in the state. I'd get you off with no problem, and give you ten thousand dollars."

The maid puts down the phone. Still listening, George hears two shots. A moment later, the maid comes back on and says, "Well, I just killed them both like you asked."

"Fine," George says. "Now I want you to take both of the bodies and throw them in the pool."

"Pool?" the maid asks. "There's no pool here."

George says, "Is this 555-6734?"

All through the movie, Dick hears annoying laughter coming from the row behind him. Finally, he's had enough. He turns in his seat and is shocked to see a German shepherd sitting next to its owner.

The angry man says to the dog's owner, "I can't believe you brought your dog here!"

"Neither can I," says the owner. "He hated the book."

Steve was making passionate love to a married woman when they both heard a car door slam in the driveway.

"Oh, my god," the cheating wife cries. "My husband! If he catches you here, he'll kill you for sure."

Grabbing his pants, Steve says, "Quick, where's the back door?"

"We don't have one," the wife says.

"Okay," Steve replies. "Then where do you want it?'

What's black and white and red all over?

A nun with multiple stab wounds.

How many Polacks does it take to rape a woman?

Three—one to hold her down and the other two to read the instructions.

"I don't know how to tell you this," the gynecologist said to the coffee shop waitress, "but you've got a tea bag stuck up your vagina!"

The waitress said. "I wonder what I served my last customer . . ."

What comes immediately after 69?

Listerine.

What's the difference between a pick-pocket and a peeping Tom?

One snatches watches, the other watches snatches.

What has four wheels and flies?

A dead cripple in a wheelchair.

What's the definition of a cheap date?

Taking an anorexic to dinner.

What's the definition of gross?

Siamese twins joined at the mouth, and one of them throws up.

How do you know when you're flying Air Mexico?

After landing, you have to steal your luggage back.

What did the nymphomaniac say when her dog started licking her face?

"Down boy!"

What's the definition of plastic surgery?

Cutting up your wife's credit cards.

A man walks into a drugstore to buy some rubbers.

"What size?" the druggist asks.

The man doesn't know, so the druggist says to him, "Don't be embarrassed, sir. We run into this problem all the time. In the back room, we have a board with several size holes in it. Try each one and tell us which one fits you best."

The man goes into the back and puts his pecker into one of the holes. What he doesn't know is, the druggist's wife is working in the back room behind the board. As the man sticks his cock into each hole, she starts toying with him until he gets harder than a rock and comes like a geyser.

A few minutes later, when he figures out his size, the man returns to the front of the store. The druggist asks him, "So, did you figure out your size?"

The man says, "The hell with the rubbers. How much do you want for that board?"

What do you call rubbers for midgets?

Condom-minimums.

"So let me ask you something," the rich man says to his mistress. "If you were to someday find yourself pregnant, broke, and abandoned, what would you do?"

"Kill myself I guess," the mistress answers.

The rich man says, "Good girl."

Why was the ninety-year-old man acquitted of rape?

The evidence wouldn't stand up in court.

How can you tell a rich Mexican?

He has two junked cars in his front yard.

How do you know when it's really cold in Washington, D.C.?

Bill actually sleeps with Hillary.

Why do the Clintons take Chelsea everywhere they go?

They don't want to have to kiss her goodbye.

Why did the Polish burglar break two windows?

One to get in, one to get out.

What do you call a guy who screws Bugs Bunny?

Elmer Fuck.

Who is the leading maker of vibrators in America?

Genital Electric.

Hear about the moron who held up a lawyer?

He lost $2000.